GUATEMALA 2016 HUMAN RIGHTS REPORT

Note: This report was updated 4/12/17; see Appendix F: Errata for more information.

EXECUTIVE SUMMARY

Guatemala is a multiparty constitutional republic. On January 14, Jimmy Morales of the National Convergence Front (FCN) party was sworn into office for a four-year term as president. International observers considered the presidential election held in 2015 as generally free and fair.

Civilian authorities at times did not maintain effective control over the security forces.

Principal human rights abuses included widespread institutional corruption, particularly in the police and judicial sectors; security force involvement in serious crimes, such as kidnapping, drug trafficking, trafficking in persons, and extortion; and societal violence, including lethal violence against women.

Other human rights problems included arbitrary or unlawful killings, abuse and mistreatment by National Civil Police (PNC) members; harsh and sometimes life-threatening prison conditions; arbitrary arrest and detention; prolonged pretrial detention; failure of the judicial system to conduct full and timely investigations and fair trials; government failure to fully protect judicial officials, witnesses, and civil society representatives from intimidation and threats; and internal displacement of persons. In addition, there was sexual harassment and discrimination against women; child abuse, including the commercial sexual exploitation of children; discrimination and abuse of persons with disabilities; and trafficking in persons and human smuggling, including of unaccompanied children. Other problems included marginalization of indigenous communities and ineffective mechanisms to address land conflicts; discrimination on the basis of sexual orientation and gender identity; and ineffective enforcement of labor and child labor laws.

The government cooperated with the UN-backed International Commission against Impunity in Guatemala (CICIG) to strengthen the rule of law and prosecute officials who committed abuses. Impunity continued to be widespread. Gangs, organized crime, and narcotics trafficking organizations committed numerous acts of violence; corruption and inadequate investigation made prosecution difficult.

Section 1. Respect for the Integrity of the Person, Including Freedom from:

a. Arbitrary Deprivation of Life and other Unlawful or Politically Motivated Killings

There were several reports that the government or its agents committed arbitrary or unlawful killings. As of August 31, the PNC and its Office of Professional Responsibility (ORP), the mechanism for investigating security force abuses, reported no complaints of homicide. The Human Rights Ombudsman's Office (PDH), however, reported one complaint of murder, and the Attorney General's Office, commonly known as the Public Ministry, reported one case of homicide, three cases of manslaughter, and one case of premeditated murder by PNC officers through August. Local media reported that a PNC officer killed a grocery store owner on January 4 in Santiago Atitlan, Solola. The trial was pending at year's end.

On October 9, authorities arrested 13 members of the military from the San Juan Sacatepequez military brigade for the alleged extrajudicial killing of Hector Donaldo Contreras Sanchez in December 2015. According to media reports, the soldiers accused Contreras of consuming marijuana and proceeded to beat him unconscious. Forensics report later found no evidence of the victim being under the influence of alcohol or drugs. The case was under Public Ministry investigation at year's end.

On January 6, the Public Ministry arrested 14 high-ranking former military officers on charges of human rights violations for hundreds of extrajudicial executions during the internal armed conflict (1990-96) at former Military Zone 21, a site currently known as the Regional Training Command for Peacekeeping Operations (CREOMPAZ) in Coban, Verapaz. The CREOMPAZ case was assigned to a high-risk court, a special court created in 2009 with competence to hear cases that pose a serious risk to the judges, the prosecutor, the defense, or any other individual involved in the case. On June 7, the court found sufficient evidence to send eight individuals to trial. On September 14, the Public Ministry appealed the exclusion of a number of charges in the proceedings. At year's end the trial date had not been confirmed.

Retrial proceedings restarted on March 16 against former head of state Efrain Rios Montt and his intelligence chief, Jose Mauricio Rodriguez Sanchez, in the case of genocide involving the Maya Ixil community. Proceedings had been suspended after the First Court of Appeals ruled that Rios Montt and Rodriguez Sanchez should be tried separately. Rios Montt had been found guilty of genocide and crimes against humanity and was originally sentenced to 80 years in prison. Later the Constitutional Court overturned the conviction on procedural grounds and returned the case to a different court for rehearing. In 2015 a high-risk court determined that Rios Montt was mentally unfit for public trial but ordered that the trial continue behind closed doors and with a guardian present. It also ruled that any verdict could be used only for the application of corrective measures on behalf of the victims and that Rios Montt cannot be sentenced to prison.

On November 16, in a different case against Rios Montt, a high-risk court dismissed a motion by the defense team to suspend criminal prosecution for genocide and crimes against humanity. The defense argued that Rios Montt was mentally unfit to stand trial. The court was scheduled to rule on February 9, 2017, on whether to send Rios Montt to trial. At year's end the retrial dates had not been set for either case.

As of December the government had paid $14.2 million in reparations to families affected by the Chixoy Hydro-Electric Dam. During the dam's construction (1975-85), more than 400 individuals died and thousands were displaced. As part of a 2014 reparations agreement, the government agreed to pay $156 million over 15 years in individual and community reparations to those who were affected.

b. Disappearance

There were no new reports of politically motivated disappearances. The government took actions to investigate and prosecute cases of forced disappearances from the internal armed conflict period (1960-96). On January 6, four high-ranking retired army officers were arrested for the 1981 forced disappearance of minor Marco Antonio Molina Theissen. On August 22, the Attorney General's Office presented new charges against retired army general Benedicto Lucas Garcia, who was also charged in the CREOMPAZ mass graves case. On October 25, a high-risk court found sufficient evidence to charge Lucas Garcia with illegal detention, torture, and sexual violence, and it accepted new charges of aggravated sexual assault for the other four defendants. The court was to determine whether all five defendants would go to trial on January 13, 2017.

c. Torture and Other Cruel, Inhuman, or Degrading Treatment or Punishment

Although the constitution and law prohibit torture and other cruel, inhuman, or degrading treatment or punishment, there were credible reports of abuse and other mistreatment by PNC members.

In October preliminary hearings, a court ordered the trial of PNC agents Carlos Baten Perez, Rogelio Perez Hernandez, Nancy Evelia Rodriguez Alai, and Cesar Augusto Funes Morales for the torture and illegal detention of four suspects in April 2015 in the Villa Nueva suburb of Guatemala City. As of November the case was in the evidentiary phase, during which the Public Ministry presents all available evidence in advance of the trial.

Prison and Detention Center Conditions

Prison conditions were harsh and potentially life threatening, with multiple instances of inmates killing other inmates. Sexual assault, inadequate sanitation and medical care, and gross overcrowding continued to place prisoners at significant risk. On July 18, prisoner Byron Lima Oliva, a former army captain, was killed, along with 12 others, inside the Pavon prison. Lima Oliva was serving a 20-year sentence for the 1998 murder of human rights defender Bishop Juan Jose Gerardi and had alleged ties to political corruption and narcotics-trafficking networks. At year's end CICIG was investigating the case.

Physical Conditions: Prison overcrowding continued to be a problem. According to the prison system registry, as of September 6, there were 20,743 inmates, including 1,974 women, held in facilities designed to hold 6,742 persons. Physical conditions including sanitation and bathing facilities, dental and medical care, ventilation, temperature control, and lighting were wholly inadequate. Prisoners had difficulty obtaining potable water, complained of inadequate food, and often had to pay for additional sustenance. Illegal drug sales and use continued to be widespread. Prison officials continued to report a loss of safety and control, including escape attempts, gang fights, inability to control the flow of contraband goods into prisons, and the fabrication of weapons. Prisoners continued to direct criminal activity both inside and outside of prisons. From January through September 5, at least 55 inmates died of unnatural causes while in prison.

Conditions for male and female prisoners were generally comparable throughout the country. Media and nongovernmental organizations (NGOs) reported that female and juvenile inmates faced continuing physical and sexual abuse. Female inmates reported unnecessary body searches and verbal abuse by prison guards. Children below age four could live in prison with their mothers, although the penitentiary system provided inadequate food for young children, and many suffered from illness. Lesbian, gay, bisexual, transgender, and intersex (LGBTI) rights groups alleged that other prisoners often sexually assaulted LGBTI individuals and that there were insufficient facilities to protect LGBTI individuals under custody. The Ministry of Government approved treatment standards for LGBTI prisoners in 2015, and NGOs trained authorities on their implementation during the year, although NGOs considered the improvements to be minimal. Occasionally authorities held pretrial detainees together with convicted prisoners, juveniles with adults, and male and female detainees together.

Media reported similar conditions of abuse and overcrowding at the four juvenile detention centers administered separately by the Secretariat of Social Welfare. In October a judge ordered the closing of the annex of one of the detention centers for one year and mandated reform of the facilities.

Administration: The government's independent Office of the Human Rights Ombudsman (PDH) and the National Office for the Prevention of Torture (NOPT), whose responsibilities include prisoner rights, received complaints and conducted oversight of the prison system. The PDH and the NOPT can submit recommendations to the prison system based on complaints. No independent agency or unit, however, had a mandate to change or implement policy or to act on behalf of prisoners and detainees. Recordkeeping remained inadequate.

While the law requires authorities to permit prisoners and detainees to submit complaints to judicial authorities without censorship and request investigation of credible allegations of inhuman conditions, authorities failed to investigate most allegations of inhuman conditions and treatment or to document the results of such investigations in a publicly accessible manner.

Independent Monitoring: The government permitted visits by local and international human rights groups, the Organization of American States (OAS), public defenders, and religious groups. The PDH and the NOPT also periodically visited prison facilities. The PDH reported it was sometimes difficult to gain access to the juvenile detention centers administered by the Secretariat of Social Welfare.

d. Arbitrary Arrest or Detention

The constitution and law prohibit arbitrary arrest and detention, but there were credible reports of extrajudicial arrests, illegal detentions, and denial of timely access to a magistrate and hearing, as required by law.

Role of the Police and Security Apparatus

The PNC, which is overseen by the Ministry of Government and headed by a director general appointed by the ministry, is responsible for law enforcement and maintenance of order in the country. The Ministry of National Defense oversees the military, which focuses primarily on operations in defense of the country, but the government also used the army in internal security and policing as permitted by the constitution.

Civilian authorities in some instances failed to maintain effective control over the PNC, and the government lacked effective mechanisms to investigate and punish abuse and corruption. Despite a 5 percent increase in its operating budget, the PNC remained understaffed, inadequately trained, and insufficiently funded, all of which substantially impeded its effectiveness.

There were reports of impunity involving security forces. In cases involving police forces, the ORP is responsible for internal investigations and the Public Ministry is responsible for external investigations. Authorities arrested approximately 272 police officials through August, similar to the previous year's rate. A Police Reform Commission, established under a previous administration, has a legal mandate to make necessary changes to reform the police forces. Under this framework the commission developed software to improve PNC information systems, including through a new automated victim support system that consolidates information from victims as soon as they interact with PNC at the police station; created a professional school for officers and a formal education policy; and provided almost all of the country's 54 Victim Support Offices with improved facilities and upgraded information systems.

During the year there were 747 complaints of police extortion and 206 for abuse of authority, compared with 31 and 856, respectively, in 2015. The PNC routinely transferred officers suspected of wrongdoing rather than investigating and punishing them.

Critics accused police of indiscriminate and illegal detentions when conducting antigang operations in some high-crime neighborhoods. Security officials allegedly arrested and imprisoned suspected gang members without warrants or on fabricated drug charges. The local press also reported police involvement in kidnappings for ransom.

On March 3, a soldier, Guilber Josue Barrios, allegedly drugged and raped a 14-year-old student at a civil-military institute administered by the Ministry of Defense. The suspect absconded, which prevented his trial from moving forward. A number of NGOs asserted that the Ministry of Defense demonstrated a lack of effective collaboration with civilian authorities to prevent this type of incident.

The ORP conducted internal investigations of misconduct by police officers. In the first eight months of the year, the ORP reported receiving 1,462 complaints alleging misconduct by police personnel.

All new PNC and military soldiers receive some training in human rights and professional ethics. During the year the Ministry of Defense elevated its Office of Human Rights to a directorate, providing it direct access to the minister; more than doubled its personnel; and conducted active outreach to human rights organizations.

The government took actions to investigate and prosecute cases of sexual abuse from the internal armed conflict period. On February 26, retired army officers Esteelmer Reyes and Heriberto Valdez were sentenced to 120 and 240 years of prison, respectively, for sexual violence and domestic and sexual slavery involving 15 indigenous women in Sepur Zarco in 1982-83.

Arrest Procedures and Treatment of Detainees

The law requires presentation of a court-issued warrant to a suspect prior to arrest unless police apprehend a suspect while in the act of committing a crime. Police may not detain a suspect for more than six hours without bringing the case before a judge. Authorities did not regularly respect this right and did not promptly inform some detainees of the charges against them. After arraigning suspects, the prosecutor generally has three months to complete the investigation and file a case in court or seek a formal extension of the detention period. The law prohibits the execution of search warrants between 6 p.m. and 6 a.m. unless the government has declared a state of siege. Judges can order house arrest for some suspects. The law provides for access to lawyers and bail for most crimes. The government provides legal representation for indigent detainees and detainees have access to family members. A judge has the discretion to determine whether bail is permissible for pretrial detainees.

<u>Arbitrary Arrest</u>: There were no reliable data on the number of arbitrary detentions, although most accounts indicated that police continued to ignore writs of habeas corpus in cases of illegal detention, particularly during neighborhood anti-gang operations.

<u>Pretrial Detention</u>: As of September 6, prison system records indicated 46 percent of prisoners were in pretrial detention. The law establishes a three-month limit for pretrial detention but authorities regularly held detainees past their legal trial or release dates. Lengthy investigations and frequent procedural motions by both defense and prosecution often led to lengthy pretrial detentions, delaying trials for months or years. Authorities did not release some prisoners after completing their full sentences due to the failure of judges to issue the necessary court order or other bureaucratic delays.

<u>Detainee's Ability to Challenge Lawfulness of Detention before a Court</u>: Suspects are entitled to challenge in court the legal basis or arbitrary nature of their detention. If successful, their release is not immediate and usually takes several days. There was no compensation for those ruled unlawfully detained.

e. Denial of Fair Public Trial

The constitution and the law provide for an independent judiciary. The judicial system failed to provide fair or timely trials due to inefficiency, corruption, insufficient personnel, and intimidation of judges, prosecutors, and witnesses.

Judges, prosecutors, plaintiffs, and witnesses continued to report threats, intimidation, and surveillance, most often from drug-trafficking organizations. By the end of September, the special prosecutor for crimes against judicial workers received 192 complaints of threats or aggression against workers in the judicial branch, compared with 202 for the same period in 2015.

CICIG assisted the Ministry of Government and Public Ministry with the investigation of cases, including allegations of extrajudicial executions, extortion, trafficking in persons, improper adoptions, corruption, and drug trafficking.

The Supreme Court continued to seek the suspension of judges and to conduct criminal investigations of improprieties or irregularities in cases under its jurisdiction. The Judicial Disciplinary Unit investigated 1,178 complaints of wrongdoing against judges, technicians, and judiciary administrative staff through

October, held hearings on 570 complaints, and applied sanctions in 360 cases, including disciplinary suspension without pay (277 cases) and recommending dismissal (34 cases).

Trial Procedures

The constitution provides for the right to a fair and public trial, the presumption of innocence, the defendant's right to be present at trial, and the right to legal counsel in a timely manner. The law requires the government to provide attorneys for defendants facing criminal charges if the defendant cannot find or afford an attorney. Defendants and their attorneys have access to government-held evidence relevant to their case and may confront adverse witnesses and present their own witnesses and evidence. The law provides for plea bargaining and the right of appeal. Three-judge panels render verdicts. The law provides for oral trials and mandates free language interpretation for those needing it; however, interpreters were not always available. Officials conduct trials in Spanish, the official language, although many citizens only speak one of the 23 officially recognized indigenous languages. The law extends the above rights to all defendants.

The Public Ministry, acting semi-independently of the executive branch, may initiate criminal proceedings on its own or in response to a complaint. Private parties may participate in the prosecution of criminal cases as plaintiffs.

Political Prisoners and Detainees

On July 22, a high-risk court released seven community leaders from Huehuetenango because kidnapping charges against them could not be substantiated. The seven had been arrested in 2015 for detaining 11 hydroelectric company workers in 2013 and had been held in preventive prison for 18 months. The court confirmed that the prisoners were community leaders or indigenous authorities mediating between the community and the hydroelectric company and expressed concern over criminalization of the rights to assemble and protest. Specifically, the presiding judge stated, "attempting to mediate a community conflict is not a crime."

Local human rights NGO Unit for the Protection of Human Rights Defenders registered 68 cases of criminalization of human rights defenders through October. Charges included defamation, legal complaint, and arbitrary detention.

Civil Judicial Procedures and Remedies

Individuals and organizations have access to administrative and judicial remedies to bring lawsuits seeking damages for, or cessation of, a human rights violation or other alleged wrongs. While the judiciary was generally impartial and independent in civil matters, it suffered from inefficiencies, excessive workload, and a legal system that often permits time-consuming but spurious complaints.

f. Arbitrary or Unlawful Interference with Privacy, Family, Home, or Correspondence

The constitution and the law prohibit such actions, and the government generally respected these prohibitions. On September 5, President Jimmy Morales dismissed Jorge Lopez, the secretary of administrative and security matters of the president, and his deputy, Cesar Sagastume, for alleged illegal surveillance. At year's end the Public Ministry was investigating their suspected involvement in the illegal monitoring of journalists, human rights defenders, business owners, and politicians. Media sources reported that former presidential advisor and current member of congress Herbert Melgar's name also appeared in the criminal complaint filed with the Public Ministry, but he continued to serve in congress and had not been formally charged.

Section 2. Respect for Civil Liberties, Including:

a. Freedom of Speech and Press

The constitution and law provide for freedom of speech and press, and the government generally respected these rights. The intimidation of journalists resulted in significant self-censorship, however.

Press and Media Freedoms: There were no legal restrictions on the editorial independence of the media. Reporters covering organized crime, including its links to corrupt public officials, acknowledged practicing self-censorship, recognizing the danger investigative journalism posed to them and their families. The independent media were active and expressed a wide variety of views, but freedom of expression advocates noted that difficulty obtaining licenses to operate community radio stations and obtaining some judicial information limited press freedom.

Violence and Harassment: Members of the press continued to report that violence and impunity impaired the practice of free and open journalism. Members of the press reported numerous threats by public officials, and criminal organizations increased journalists' sense of vulnerability. Guatemala City mayor (and former Guatemalan president) Alvaro Arzu made the following comment in a high-profile public forum on July 27, "A former president of Mexico once said that the press is either bribed or beaten. I prefer the second option."

On June 25 in Coatepeque, unidentified assailants shot and killed Alvaro Alfredo Aceytuno Lopez, a radio journalist who often reported on local governance issues. One month later, his daughter, Lindaura Aceytuno, was shot and killed in an attack that also left his 13-year-old granddaughter injured. No arrests were made, but the investigation continued at year's end.

According to the Public Ministry, 87 complaints were filed for attacks or threats against journalists, and eight journalists were killed through the middle of November, compared with 133 complaints and four killings in all of 2015. Civil society analysts attributed the increase in killings chiefly to the general state of violence in the country. The decrease in attacks or threats against journalists was also partially attributed to 2015 being a general election year and a time of significant political instability. On November 22, a Mazatenango court convicted two men and sentenced each of them to 25 years in prison for the murder of journalist Guido Armando Geovani Villatoro Ramos in March 2015.

The Public Ministry employed a unit dedicated to the investigation of threats and attacks against journalists. The NGO Center for Reporting in Guatemala noted that the unit had few resources.

Civil society organizations reported that sexual harassment of female journalists was widespread but rarely reported.

<u>Censorship or Content Restrictions</u>: Members of the press reported receiving pressure, threats, and retribution from various public officials regarding the content of their reporting. Some owners and members of media also accused the government of following a discriminatory advertising policy that penalized or rewarded print and broadcast media based upon whether the government perceived the news or commentary as supportive or critical.

In September a videographer for the media outlet *Nuevo Mundo* was fired after he took pictures of President Morales apparently sleeping at a government event. The outlet claimed it fired him because he shared the pictures without editorial permission, but the videographer claimed to have evidence to the contrary. The PDH was investigating the motives for the videographer's dismissal.

Libel/Slander Laws: In June reporter Pavel Vega from the daily newspaper *El Periodico* attempted to interview Viviana Quinonez Paiz, legal representative of TVQ--a public relations firm with close ties to the local Guatemala City government--regarding municipal contracts TVQ received as the lone bidder. She refused the interview and accused Vega of psychological harassment, citing the Law Against Femicide and Other Violence Against Women (Femicide Law). A judge subsequently issued a restraining order against the reporter for three months, prohibiting him from approaching Quinonez. The human rights ombudsman stated the harassment charges should never have been given credence in view of the lack of relationship between the two, as well as the fact that the reporter's only action was to call Quinonez' office to ask for an interview. On July 5, Quinonez filed charges against the reporter for slander and defamation for his articles related to municipal contracts awarded to TVQ. The case was pending at year's end. Journalist associations stated that use of the Femicide Law to infringe upon press freedoms set a dangerous precedent but also noted that there were relatively few cases of the law being used in this manner.

Nongovernmental Impact: Organized crime exerted influence over media outlets and reporters, frequently threatening individuals for reporting on criminal activities.

Internet Freedom

The government did not restrict or disrupt access to the internet or censor online content, and there were no credible reports the government monitored private online communications without appropriate legal authority.

Journalists expressed concern that government officials may have used twitter accounts to harass those critical of the administration and its policies. According to the International Telecommunication Union, 27 percent of the population used the internet in 2015.

Academic Freedom and Cultural Events

There were no government restrictions on academic freedom or cultural events.

b. Freedom of Peaceful Assembly and Association

The constitution provides for the freedoms of assembly and association, and the government generally respected these rights. In September the government issued a 15-day emergency decree that gave it the power to dissolve groups, meetings, protests, and media coverage that "contributed to or incited" disruption of public order. The decree was rescinded two days later after harsh reactions from many sectors of society, including the president of congress and the human rights ombudsman. The NGO Center for Legal Action on Environment (CALAS) and the National Unity of Hope party charged the executive branch with violating the constitution and abuse of power. The Supreme Court dismissed the charges on November 2; CALAS planned to appeal the decision.

Freedom of Association

The law provides for freedom of association, and the government generally respected this right. There were reports, however, of significant barriers to organizing in the labor sector (see section 7.a.).

c. Freedom of Religion

See the Department of State's *International Religious Freedom Report* at www.state.gov/religiousfreedomreport/.

d. Freedom of Movement, Internally Displaced Persons, Protection of Refugees, and Stateless Persons

The constitution and the law provide for freedom of internal movement, foreign travel, emigration, and repatriation, and the government generally respected these rights. A migration law passed in September overhauled the country's migration system and defined the term "refugee" as well as listing refugees' rights in accordance with international instruments. The process for creating new migration regulations to implement the law, which would contain greater detail on the refugee application process and refugee rights, was underway at year's end.

The government cooperated with the Office of the UN High Commissioner for Refugees (UNHCR) and other humanitarian organizations in providing protection and assistance to refugees, returning refugees, asylum seekers, stateless persons, or other persons of concern.

Internally Displaced Persons

The country does not have laws in place to protect internally displaced persons (IDPs) in line with the UN Guiding Principles on Internal Displacement. UNHCR expressed concern about the internal displacement of persons in the country due to violence, and strengthened its presence to monitor the problem and provide assistance to the displaced. The country does not officially recognize the existence of IDPs within its borders, with the exception of those displaced by climate change. Despite the fact that it did not officially recognize them as IDPs, the government provided food aid and several plots of land for the resettlement of some victims of forced displacement in the Polochic region. Civil society organizations criticized the quality of the food aid.

Protection of Refugees

Access to Asylum: The laws provide for the granting of asylum or refugee status, and the government has established a system for providing protection to refugees. The country approved 42 refugee applications from January through August. UNHCR, however, reported that identification and referral mechanisms for potential asylum seekers were inadequate. Both migration and police authorities lacked awareness of the rules for establishing refugee status.

UNHCR reported that access to education for refugees was challenging due to the country's sometimes onerous requirements for access to formal education, including documentation from the country of origin.

Section 3. Freedom to Participate in the Political Process

The constitution provides citizens the ability to choose their government in free and fair periodic elections held by secret ballot and based on nearly universal and equal suffrage for those ages 18 and older. Members of the armed forces, police, and incarcerated individuals are not eligible to vote. Electoral Law reforms enacted during the year would permit absentee and overseas voting in subsequent elections, but funding for implementation had not been budgeted.

Elections and Political Participation

Recent Elections: In 2015 Jimmy Morales of the FCN party defeated National Unity of Hope candidate Sandra Torres by 67.4 to 32.3 percent in a second round of voting and was sworn in as president on January 14. An OAS international election observation mission characterized the elections as generally free and fair.

The Attorney General's Office continued to investigate allegations of illicit campaign financing in the 2015 elections. The Supreme Electoral Court cancelled former presidential candidate Manuel Baldizon's party, LIDER (Democratic Liberty Renewed), in February for campaign law violations. LIDER was appealing the decision.

<u>Participation of Women and Minorities</u>: The law provides the rights of women and minorities to vote, run for office, serve as electoral monitors, and otherwise participate in political life. Traditional and cultural practices, however, limited the political participation of women and members of indigenous groups.

Twenty-four women served in the 158-seat Congress, and there were two women in the 14-member cabinet. Seven women served on the 13-member Supreme Court, and five women served on the 10-member Constitutional Court--the most women in either court's history.

While the indigenous population constituted 44 percent of the population, according to the latest 2002 government census, indigenous representation in national government was minimal. There was one indigenous member in the cabinet, one on the Constitutional Court, and one on the Supreme Court. There were approximately 20 indigenous members of Congress. Indigenous individuals comprised a larger share of elected local government officials, filling 113 of the 333 mayoral seats elected in 2015.

Section 4. Corruption and Lack of Transparency in Government

The law provides criminal penalties for official corruption, but officials frequently engaged in corrupt practices with impunity. There were numerous reports of government corruption during the year, many of which the Public Ministry and CICIG investigated and prosecuted on charges including money laundering, illegal political party financing, and bribery.

<u>Corruption</u>: The Comptroller General's Office and the Public Ministry are responsible for combating corruption. The comptroller general's mandate is to monitor public spending, and the attorney general's mandate is to prosecute related crimes. Although both agencies actively collaborated with civil society and were relatively independent, they lacked adequate resources, which affected their ability to carry out their mandates.

On June 2, the Public Ministry accused former president Otto Perez Molina and former vice president Roxana Baldetti of money laundering and illegal political party financing. The Public Ministry/CICIG investigation eventually linked the case to additional charges against the former ministers of defense, government, energy and mines, and communications for using illicit funds to provide lavish gifts to Perez Molina and Baldetti. The government issued approximately 70 arrest warrants targeting former government officials and the highest levels of the banking, state procurement, telecommunications, media, construction, agricultural, and pharmaceutical sectors. On August 4, a high-risk court sent 28 defendants who were deemed a flight risk to pretrial detention and ordered house arrest for 19 more. Perez Molina and Baldetti were in pretrial detention since 2015.

On September 13, President Morales announced that his son Jose Manuel Morales and brother Sammy Morales would cooperate in a corruption investigation based on the allegation that they procured false invoices in 2013. The case involved former public registrar Anabella de Leon, who allegedly used these invoices in a corruption scheme that defrauded the government through phony contracts.

Financial Disclosure: Public officials who earn more than 8,000 quetzals ($1,064) per month or who manage public funds are subject to financial disclosure laws overseen and enforced by the Comptroller General's Office. The financial disclosures were available to the public upon request. Administrative and criminal sanctions apply for inadequate or falsified disclosures of assets.

Public Access to Information: The law provides for the right of citizens to access public information and establishes fines for government agencies that obstruct such access. The disclosure law contains exceptions for national security, sets reasonably short timelines for disclosure, and allows for a reasonable processing fee. There are no sanctions for noncompliance. The government granted access to public information for citizens and noncitizens, including foreign media, although at times in a slow and incomplete manner. Human rights groups criticized the delay by the Ministry of Defense in releasing information related to transitional justice cases. While there was no formal mechanism to appeal denials of requests, petitioners often successfully appealed to the Office of the Human Rights Ombudsman for assistance relating to a government denial of public information.

Section 5. Governmental Attitude Regarding International and Nongovernmental Investigation of Alleged Violations of Human Rights

A variety of domestic and international human rights groups generally operated without government restriction, investigating and publishing their findings on human rights cases. Government officials were often cooperative and responsive to their views.

A number of NGOs, human rights workers, and trade unionists reported threats, violence, and intimidation. NGOs asserted the government did little to investigate these reports or to prevent further incidents. NGOs also reported the government used threats of legal action as a form of intimidation.

The Office of the Special Prosecutor for Human Rights failed to investigate the majority of complaints in a timely manner. Other cases languished in the court system.

Local human rights NGO Unit for the Protection of Human Rights Defenders reported 14 killings of human rights defenders through November 30, compared with 12 killings in all of 2015. The NGO also reported 205 attacks against human rights defenders through October, compared with 493 attacks in all of 2015. According to various human rights NGOs, many of the attacks related to land disputes and exploitation of natural resources.

Government Human Rights Bodies: The Office of the Human Rights Ombudsman monitors the human rights set forth in the constitution and reports to Congress. The ombudsman operated with government cooperation and issued public reports and recommendations, including an annual report to Congress on the fulfillment of its mandate. The office lacked adequate resources.

The President's Commission on Human Rights (COPREDEH) has responsibility to formulate and promote the government's human rights policy. COPREDEH also led coordination of police protection for various human rights and labor activists. COPREDEH generally benefited from the administration's cooperation and operated without political or party interference. In August, however, the Solicitor General's Office challenged COPREDEH's authority to represent the government in human rights matters before international institutions. In September the president issued an executive decree giving COPREDEH this authority. Resources for the commission were not adequate for compliance with CIDH recommendations and reparation rulings.

The Congressional Committee on Human Rights drafts and provides advice on legislation regarding human rights. The law requires all political parties represented in Congress to have a representative on the committee. NGOs considered the committee to be an effective public forum for promoting and protecting human rights.

Section 6. Discrimination, Societal Abuses, and Trafficking in Persons

Women

Rape and Domestic Violence: The law criminalizes rape, including spousal rape, and sets penalties between five and 50 years in prison. Police had minimal training or capacity to investigate sexual crimes or assist survivors of such crimes, and the government did not enforce the law effectively. The PDH Ombudsman for Women and activists agreed that full investigation and prosecution of domestic violence and rape cases took an average of two to three years if the victims had access to quality legal representation. Impunity for perpetrators remained very high. Rape survivors frequently did not report crimes due to lack of confidence in the justice system, social stigma, and fear of reprisal.

Rape and other sexual offenses remained serious problems. According to the Public Ministry, there were 11,399 reports of sexual or physical assault through August. During the same period, there were 610 convictions for sexual or physical assault on women, an increase from the 527 convictions in the same period the previous year.

The government took steps to combat femicide and violence against women. The PNC's Special Unit for Sex Crimes, the Office of Attention to Victims, the Office of the Special Prosecutor for Crimes against Women, and a special unit for trafficking in persons and illegal adoptions within the Special Prosecutor's Office for Organized Crime deal with various aspects of violence against women. The judiciary maintained a 24-hour court in Guatemala City to offer services related to violence directed toward women, including sexual assault, exploitation, and trafficking of women and children. The judiciary also operated specialized courts for violence against women throughout the country, but not in every department. In September 2015 the government relaunched the Office of the Coordinator for the Prevention of Domestic Violence and Violence Against Women (CONAPREVI), which serves as the domestic violence interagency coordinator and includes several civil society organizations. CONAPREVI had been active under previous governments but was dormant in recent years due to a lack of leadership and funding.

The law establishes penalties of five to eight years for physical, economic, and psychological violence committed against women because of their gender, but violence against women, including domestic violence, remained a serious problem. The law prohibits domestic abuse, allows for the issuance of restraining orders against alleged aggressors and police protection for victims, and requires the PNC to intervene in violent situations in the home. The PNC often failed to respond to requests for assistance related to domestic violence, however, and women's rights advocates reported that few officers received training to deal with domestic violence or to assist survivors.

On November 22, the Public Ministry established a special prosecutor for femicide. The Institute of Public Criminal Defense, a government institution, provided free legal, medical, and psychological assistance to survivors of domestic violence. Femicide remained a significant problem. Sexual assault, torture, and mutilation were frequently evident in killings. The NGO Mutual Support Group, using government data, reported 565 violent deaths of women through the end of September. As of that month, authorities convicted 56 individuals for femicide. NGOs expressed concern that sentences were sometimes lenient.

Sexual and domestic violence remained serious problems. The PDH Office of Ombudsman for Women supported survivors of domestic and social violence by accompanying them to judicial proceedings and offering some social services such as psychological support. The Office of Ombudsman for Indigenous Women also coordinated and promoted action by government institutions and NGOs to prevent violence and discrimination against indigenous women, but lacked resources to reach all areas. The office maintained no statistics on its caseload. Civil society organizations provided mediation and free legal services to low-income women.

Although the law affords protection, including shelter, to victims of domestic violence, there were insufficient facilities for this purpose. The Ministry of Government operated eight shelters for survivors of abuse in departments with the greatest incidence of domestic violence. Due to continual budget uncertainties, the shelters' operations were erratic. Several shelters funded by private donors or municipal governments operated in cities and the countryside. Many of the centers provided legal and psychological support and temporary accommodation.

Sexual Harassment: No single law, including laws against sexual violence, deals directly with sexual harassment, although several laws refer to it, such as the Femicide Law. There were no reliable estimates of the frequency of sexual harassment; however, human rights organizations reported sexual harassment was widespread. The government ran a pilot program consisting of social media and bus advertisements to promote greater awareness against sexual harassment and to encourage victims and witnesses to report the crime. Under this pilot program, the PNC, local transit police, and other groups established protocols for handling sexual harassment complaints.

Reproductive Rights: Couples and individuals have the right to decide the number, spacing, and timing of their children and to manage their reproductive health, free from discrimination, coercion, and violence. They did not always have the information and means to do so.

Cultural, geographic, and linguistic barriers hampered access to reproductive health care, particularly for indigenous women in rural areas. Discriminatory attitudes among health-care providers and a lack of culturally sensitive reproductive and maternal health-care services deterred many indigenous women from accessing these services.

As a result of efforts to expand health services to underserved communities, the government was able to decrease the maternal mortality ratio and increase the percentage of institutional deliveries. Although the country made progress towards decreasing the maternal mortality ratio, it remained relatively high at 88 deaths per 100,000 live births. The UN Population Fund (UNFPA) reported in 2016 that skilled health personnel attended only 66 percent of births. Unsafe abortion also contributed to the country's high maternal mortality ratio; legal abortion was tightly restricted except to save the life of the mother.

Discrimination: Although the law establishes the principle of gender equality and criminalizes discrimination, women faced discrimination, particularly under family and labor law, and were less likely to hold management positions. The government's Secretariat for Women's Affairs advises the president on interagency coordination of policies affecting women and their development.

Women were employed primarily in low-wage jobs in agriculture, retail businesses, the service sector, textile and apparel industries, and government. Women also obtained employment more frequently in the informal sector, where pay was generally lower and benefits nonexistent. The 2015 *Global Gender Gap Report* estimated women's earned income was 56 percent that of men, and women on average received 64 percent of men's salaries for comparable work. Many women engaged in agricultural work and often reported receiving less than 50 percent of a man's salary for similar work. Women may legally own, manage, and inherit property on an equal basis with men, including in situations involving divorce.

Economic violence is a crime under the femicide law. The law defines it as actions that deprive a woman of the economic benefits to which she is legally entitled and cause damage to her economic situation. The crime occurs most frequently during divorce when a husband refuses to pay alimony, cancels or liquidates bank accounts, or sells jointly owned property without the spouse's knowledge. A slow court system and late notifications of legal actions or notifications in Spanish to women who could not read Spanish contributed to the situation. According to the Public Ministry, from January through September, 271 reports of economic violence were filed, and authorities obtained five convictions.

Children

Birth Registration: Children derive citizenship by birth within the country's territory or from their parents. UNICEF described low birth registration as a "serious problem," and UNHCR reported problems in registering births were especially acute in indigenous communities due to inadequate government registration and documentation systems. Factors such as the need to travel to unfamiliar urban areas, to interact with nonindigenous male government officials, and to speak Spanish inhibited some indigenous women from registering their children. Authorities prevented foreign citizens residing in the country without appropriate documentation from registering their locally born children prior to regularizing their own immigration status. Lack of registration restricted children's access to some public services and created conditions that could lead to statelessness.

Education: While compulsory through age 14, education through the secondary level is not obligatory, and less than half of eligible children attended secondary school. Also, less than half of secondary schools were public. Girls, especially girls in indigenous communities, were significantly less likely than boys to be educated to the secondary school level. Access to compulsory education in primary school was limited in many rural areas.

Child Abuse: Child abuse remained a serious problem. In March the country created the unit of Special Prosecutor for Crimes against Children and Adolescents. A unit under the Special Prosecutor for Crimes against Women had previously handled child abuse cases. The Public Ministry reported that it convicted the abusers of 489 minor victims for sexual abuse or other types of violence through September.

According to the Secretariat against Sexual Violence, Exploitation, and Trafficking in Persons (SVET), from January through July, 1,552 cases of pregnancies of minors 14 years old or younger were recorded nationwide, with the majority of cases coming from the departments of Huehuetenango, Alta Verapaz, Guatemala, San Marcos, and Peten. The secretary estimated that 80 percent of these cases were due to intrafamily sexual abuse. SVET launched a press campaign with special events and training sessions in rural areas to combat pregnancy of minors.

The Secretariat of Social Welfare, which oversees children's treatment, training, special education, and welfare programs, provided shelter and assistance to children who were victims of abuse but sometimes placed children in shelters with juveniles who had criminal records. The government operated a shelter for minor victims of violence, abandonment, and exploitation in San Jose Pinula and in two temporary shelters in Quetzaltenango and Zacapa. SVET had shelters for victims of human trafficking and sexual violence in Coatepeque, Coban, and Guatemala City.

Early and Forced Marriage: The legal age for marriage is 18. In 2015 Congress eliminated a provision that previously allowed girls to marry at 14 and boys at 16 with parental consent. There were reports of forced early marriages in some rural indigenous communities. UNICEF reported that 30 percent of women 20 to 24 years of age were first married or in union by age 18 (7 percent of them by age 15) between 2008 and 2014. In an effort to identify cases of early and forced marriage, the government instituted nationwide training programs and protocols to encourage public employees to report pregnancies and childbirth among underage mothers.

The NGO Childhood Refuge reported an estimated 15,000 irregular marriages of minors had occurred since 2015, 70 percent of which took place in the western part of the country. Given the change in law raising the minimum age for marriage, the NGO also reported an increase of informal unions involving minors, which essentially functioned as marriages.

Sexual Exploitation of Children: The law provides sentences ranging from 13 to 24 years in prison, depending on the victim's age, for engaging in sex with a minor. The minimum age of consensual sex is 18. The Public Ministry reported several complaints of sexual assault or rape against minors and successfully prosecuted some aggressors. The Ministry's Office of Trafficking increased the number of investigators and prosecutors to respond to the sexual exploitation of minors, including opening an office dedicated to cybercrime. SVET broadened its coordination role by engaging directly with municipal governments and mayors to educate them on combatting sexual abuse, child abuse, and trafficking.

The law prohibits child pornography and establishes penalties of six to 10 years in prison for producing, promoting, and selling child pornography and two to four years' imprisonment for possessing it. The Public Ministry and PNC conducted several raids against alleged online child pornography networks. The commercial sexual exploitation of children, including child sex tourism, remained a problem, with credible reports of child sex tourism in Antigua, Guatemala City, and the Department of Solola.

According to figures for 2016 released by the Public Ministry's Office of Special Prosecutor for Children, authorities received 5,257 reports of sexual violence against minors and youth up to 19 years of age by mid-September. It received 47 reports of sexual exploitation involving minors and 141 reports of trafficking in persons.

<u>Displaced Children</u>: Criminals and gangs often recruited street children, many of them victims of domestic abuse, for purposes of stealing, transporting contraband, prostitution, and conducting illegal drug activities. According to law enforcement sources, there were approximately 15,500 Barrio 18 gang members and 13,950 Mara Salvatrucha gang members. The NGO Mutual Support Group reported that 74 minors suffered violent deaths nationwide between January and March, a significant increase from 2015. NGOs dealing with gangs and other youth reported that youth detained by police were subject to abusive treatment, including physical assaults.

A significant number of unaccompanied children attempted to leave the country. Polling indicated that the primary motivations for migration were a lack of economic and educational opportunity in the country, fear of violence, and family reunification. NGOs reported that the Secretariat of Social Welfare (SBS), which is responsible for the care of both returned migrant children and unaccompanied foreign migrant children, reported two cases of sexual abuse of children under its care during the year. The cases highlighted the persistent problem of overcrowding in shelters, along with security issues. For instance, according to PDH, 44 minors disappeared from secured SBS shelters from September to mid-November. One NGO provided shelter and comprehensive social services for unaccompanied foreign migrant children.

<u>International Child Abductions</u>: The country is a party to the 1980 Hague Convention on the Civil Aspects of International Child Abduction. See the Department of State's *Annual Report on International Parental Child Abduction* at travel.state.gov/content/childabduction/en/legal/compliance.html.

Anti-Semitism

The Jewish population numbered approximately 1,500 persons. During a May protest against Energuate, a power distribution company purchased in December 2015 by a company with connections to Israel, protesters used a banner that had an image of Jesus Christ and stated, "Jews killed me on the cross. Now Jews from Energuate are killing my people in Guatemala with energy." Jewish community leaders filed a complaint with the PDH, which pursued the case in court. During the summer the protesting group and the Jewish community settled the matter out of court with a formal apology from the protesting group.

In June the former mayor of San Juan La Laguna, Antonio Adolfo Perez y Perez, was placed under house arrest during his trial for abuse of authority and discrimination for his involvement in the expulsion of members of the ultraorthodox Jewish sect Lev Tahor in 2014.

In September authorities raided the homes of the Lev Tahor community in Guatemala City. Authorities stated they were investigating reports of child abuse; however, they found no evidence. Lev Tahor members claimed they were persecuted because of their faith.

Trafficking in Persons

Late in 2015 Congress passed an antihuman smuggling law that designated migration-related smuggling as a crime. See also the Department of State's *Trafficking in Persons Report* at www.state.gov/j/tip/rls/tiprpt/.

Persons with Disabilities

The constitution contains no specific prohibitions against discrimination based on physical, sensory, intellectual, and mental disabilities in employment, education, access to health care, or the provision of other state services. The law, however, mandates equal access to public facilities and provides some other legal protections. In many cases, however, the law was not enforced. The law does not mandate that persons with disabilities have access to information or communications. The government devoted few resources to addressing the needs of persons with disabilities.

The National Council for Persons with Disabilities reported that few persons with disabilities attended educational institutions or held jobs. The council, composed of representatives of relevant government ministries and agencies, is the principal government entity responsible for protecting the rights of persons with disabilities. There were minimal educational resources for persons with disabilities. Most universities did not have facilities accessible to persons with disabilities. The Social Development Ministry had 23 employees with disabilities, but other ministries had very few, or no, such employees. During the year a previously ad hoc congressional committee on disabilities became permanent.

The National Council for Persons with Disabilities began a nationwide survey to estimate the number of persons with disabilities. It also signed cooperation agreements with various ministries including the Public Ministry and the Secretariat of Women's Issues to address the needs of persons with disabilities in their infrastructure, services, and programs.

The Federico Mora National Hospital for Mental Health, the only public health provider for persons with mental illness, lacked basic supplies, equipment, hygienic living conditions, and adequate professional staff. It fired several employees in 2015 after disability advocates and media reported mistreatment of residents, including physical, psychological, and sexual violence by other residents, guards, and hospital staff, especially with respect to women and children with disabilities. Despite the staff changes, disability rights organizations noted little else had changed.

Indigenous People

The government's National Institute of Statistics estimated that indigenous persons from 22 ethnic groups comprised 44 percent of the population. Many experts believed the number was considerably higher. The law provides for equal rights for indigenous persons and obliges the government to recognize, respect, and promote the lifestyles, customs, traditions, social organizations, and manner of dress of indigenous persons. The government does not recognize particular indigenous groups as having a special legal status under national law.

Indigenous representatives claimed that actors in a number of regional development projects failed to consult meaningfully with local communities. In some cases indigenous communities were not regularly or adequately consulted or able to participate in decisions affecting the exploitation of resources in their communities, including energy, minerals, timber, rivers, or other natural resources. They also lacked effective mechanisms for dialogue with the state to resolve conflicts. During the year courts suspended the operating licenses of several hydroelectric and mining projects for not complying with requirements for consultations with indigenous communities as required under International Labor Organization Convention (ILO) 169, recognizing the convention's requirement that the government must play a role in the process. Previously, businesses had carried out consultations independently without government oversight. The government was working to design a more thorough consultations process consistent with ILO standards.

Indigenous communities continued to report a lack of public infrastructure investment in their communities, resulting in poor roads and limited access to running water and electricity. Indigenous persons reported the need for schools with bilingual (i.e., Spanish and their indigenous language) education and cultural studies; educational scholarships; leadership training to increase indigenous persons' participation in politics; and the construction of universities (not only extension campuses), hospitals, and health clinics in their communities.

Indigenous communities were underrepresented in national politics and remained largely outside the political, economic, social, and cultural mainstream. This was mainly due to limited educational opportunities (contrary to law), limited communication regarding their rights, and pervasive discrimination. These factors contributed to continued disproportionate poverty among most indigenous populations.

In April the governor of Alta Verapaz, Estela Ventura, who is of indigenous descent, filed a criminal complaint against eight members of Congress on the grounds of harassment, racial discrimination, and influence peddling. The governor claimed to have recordings in which the representatives used racial slurs against her in a meeting. On August 31, a judge agreed to remove immunity for the eight representatives in order to open a full investigation.

Indigenous lands lacked effective demarcation, making the legal recognition of titles to the land problematic. Indigenous rights advocates asserted that pervasive ignorance by security authorities of indigenous norms and practices engendered misunderstandings. The government located three police academies in largely indigenous areas of the country to increase the number of indigenous police officers and assign them to work within their own ethnic or linguistic communities.

The Department of Indigenous People in the Ministry of Labor, tasked with investigating cases of discrimination and representing indigenous rights, counseled indigenous persons on their rights. Limited resources hindered the department's effectiveness. Indigenous persons were particularly vulnerable to labor trafficking.

The justice system significantly increased the number of legally mandated court interpreters for criminal proceedings and reported that it held 8,000 court proceedings in Mayan languages through August. Despite the increase, availability did not meet demand.

Acts of Violence, Discrimination, and Other Abuses Based on Sexual Orientation and Gender Identity

The country's antidiscrimination laws do not apply to LGBTI individuals. LGBTI rights groups alleged that police officers regularly engaged in extortion and harassed male and transgender individuals they believed to be sex workers. There was general societal discrimination against LGBTI persons in access to education, health care, employment, and housing. The government undertook minimal efforts to address this discrimination. After being elected as president of the country's first congressional women's caucus in September, the first openly lesbian member of Congress, Sandra Moran, was subject to discrimination in the form of an online petition that demanded her removal due to her LGBTI status. Moran filed a complaint with the PDH.

According to LGBTI rights groups, gay and transgender individuals often experienced police abuse. A lack of trust in the judicial system and a fear of further harassment or social recrimination discouraged victims from filing complaints. NGOs conducted sensitization training classes with police officials but noted that the number of trained officials remained low. The National Police and Public Ministry changed their complaint registration systems to include a field identifying whether the complainant is a member of the LGBTI community. Due to general fears of discrimination, few LGBTI community members were comfortable self-identifying to officials.

LGBTI groups claimed that women experienced specific forms of discrimination such as forced marriages and forced pregnancies through so-called corrective rape, although these incidents were rarely, if ever, reported to authorities.

The Public Ministry and SVET took up the first case of trafficking in persons involving transgender individuals, rescuing and treating several victims and returning them to their home countries. The National Registry circulated an internal memo on nondiscrimination against the LGBTI community, although officials still barred transgender individuals from obtaining identification documents that reflected a different gender. Transgender individuals continued to face severe discrimination.

HIV and AIDS Social Stigma

The law does not expressly include HIV/AIDS status among the categories prohibited from discrimination. There was societal discrimination against persons with HIV/AIDS. Forms of discrimination included being required by government authorities to reveal HIV/AIDS test results to receive certain public benefits or from employers in order to be hired. In addition, HIV/AIDS patients experienced discrimination from medical personnel when receiving treatment in public hospitals and had their right to confidentiality violated by disclosure of their status. Discrimination against LGBTI persons with HIV/AIDS was particularly pronounced and affected their access to HIV-prevention programs.

Other Societal Violence or Discrimination

Several times vigilante mobs attacked and killed those suspected of crimes such as rape, kidnapping, theft, or extortion. The NGO Mutual Support Group reported that in the first three months of the year, five persons were killed in public lynchings, and 26 were injured. Many observers attributed the acts to public frustration with the failure of police and judicial authorities to provide justice and security. As a result local citizen security groups were formed and operated autonomously. In many instances PNC agents feared for their own safety and refused to intervene. In August a mob in Patulul set fire to and killed a man arrested as an alleged extortionist who had participated in the shooting of a microbus driver.

Section 7. Worker Rights

a. Freedom of Association and the Right to Collective Bargaining

The law provides for the right of workers, with the exception of security force members, to form and join trade unions of their choice, conduct legal strikes, and bargain collectively. The law, however, places some restrictions on these rights. For instance, legal recognition of a new industrywide union requires that the membership constitute a majority of the workers in an industry and restricts union leadership to citizens. The law prohibits antiunion discrimination and employer interference in union activities and requires employers to reinstate workers dismissed for organizing union activities. A strike must have the support of the majority of a company's workforce.

The president and cabinet may suspend any strike deemed "gravely prejudicial to the country's essential activities and public services." The government defined "essential services" more broadly than international standards, thus denying the right to strike to a large number of public workers, such as those working in education, postal services, transport, and the production, transportation, and distribution of energy. Public employees may address grievances by means of conciliation for collective disputes and arbitration directly through the labor courts. For sectors considered essential, arbitration is compulsory if there is no agreement after 30 days of conciliation.

The law prohibits employer retaliation against workers engaged in legal strikes. If authorities do not recognize a strike as legal, employers may suspend or terminate workers for absence without leave. A factory or business owner is not obligated to negotiate a collective bargaining agreement unless at least 25 percent of workers in the factory or business are union members and request negotiations.

The government did not effectively enforce the law. Due in part to inadequate allocation of resources and inefficient legal and administrative processes, government institutions, such as the Ministry of Labor and the labor courts, did not effectively investigate, prosecute, or punish employers who violated freedom of association and collective bargaining laws or reinstate workers illegally dismissed for engaging in union activities. Inspectors failed to take effective action to gain access to worksites in response to employers' refusal to permit labor inspectors entry to facilities to investigate worker complaints, including failing to regularly seek police assistance as required. Penalties for labor law violations range from two to 18 minimum monthly salaries ($665 to $6,000), but the penalties were inadequate and rarely enforced.

The Labor Ministry cannot impose fines or otherwise sanction employers for labor law violations discovered during inspections. It must instead refer the cases to the labor court. Employers frequently refused to respect court decisions favorable to workers and were rarely sanctioned for doing so. Reinstatement proceedings were frequently prolonged due to appeals and employers' widespread use of tactics such as reincorporation as a different entity. For example, courts faced difficulties in providing notification of their orders when employers listed incorrect addresses or refused access to the court official delivering notification. The length of time to process cases for the reinstatement of workers and other labor law violations was excessive, often taking two to four years and sometimes lasting more than 10 years.

The Special Prosecutor's Unit for Crimes against Unionists within the Office of the Special Prosecutor for Human Rights in the Public Ministry was responsible for investigating attacks and threats against union members as well as for noncompliance with judicial orders in labor cases. Staffing for the unit increased from five in 2014 to 12 (two prosecutors, eight assistant prosecutors, and two administrators). According to Public Ministry statistics, the unit won two convictions in cases involving violence against union members. CICIG highlighted several factors that negatively affected investigations, including a lack of methodological planning and continuity between the prosecutors handling the case; delays in conducting the criminal investigation; and witnesses' fear of making declarations. The government reported that, of 2,312 cases referred (including a backlog from previous years), only eight resulted in convictions, with the vast majority of cases still under investigation.

The Ministry of Government operated a personal protection program that included some trade unionists. The ministry reported that one union member received personal security protection measures during the year, and 45 received perimeter security measures. The ministry enacted a Protocol for the Implementation of Immediate and Preventive Security Measures for Human Rights Activists in 2014, but trade union confederations and the ILO indicated there was minimal progress toward ensuring the protection of threatened trade union officials and members. Local unions continued to urge authorities to investigate the killings of unionists and called for increased personal security for union leaders and members.

In 2015 the government, together with employer and worker representatives, agreed to a plan to avoid the establishment of an ILO Commission of Inquiry, based on a complaint filed in 2012 alleging that the government had not complied with ILO Convention 87. During the year the government took some steps to implement the plan, including setting up a hotline to enable labor activists to report violence, and continuing to convene the Trade Union Committee of the Public Prosecutor's Office to monitor progress on investigations into violence.

Nevertheless, the ILO noted the need for additional urgent action in several areas, including investigation and prosecution of perpetrators of trade union violence; the adoption of protection measures for union officials and members at no cost to union members; legislative reforms to remove obstacles to freedom of association and the right to strike; and raising awareness of the rights to freedom of association and collective bargaining, particularly in the apparel and textile industries. The ILO also called for greater compliance with reinstatement orders in cases of antiunion dismissals. Separately, in June 2015 an arbitral panel under the Dominican Republic-Central America-United States Free Trade Agreement conducted a hearing regarding the government's failure to enforce its labor laws effectively. During its November session, noting positive steps taken to date, the ILO Governing Body deferred decision on establishing a Commission of Inquiry. The arbitral panel decision was pending at year's end.

Violence and threats against trade unionists and labor activists remained serious problems. Authorities did not thoroughly investigate most acts of violence and threats, and they went unprosecuted. Several labor leaders reported death threats and other acts of intimidation.

Procedural hurdles, union formation restrictions, and impunity for employers refusing to receive or ignoring court orders limited freedom of association and collective bargaining. Government statistics on attempted union registrations indicated that most registrations were rejected. Employers routinely resisted union formation attempts, delayed or only partially complied with agreements resulting from direct negotiations, and ignored judicial rulings requiring the employer to negotiate with recognized unions. There were credible reports of retaliation by employers against workers who tried to exercise their rights, including numerous complaints filed with the Ministry of Labor and the Public Ministry alleging employer retaliation for union activity. Common practices included termination and harassment of workers who attempted to form unions, creation of illegal company-supported unions to counter legally established unions, blacklisting of union organizers, and threats of factory closures. If workers joined a union or refused to disaffiliate, employers threatened not to renew their contracts or offer subcontracted workers permanent employment.

There continued to be reports that management or their agents harassed and threatened workers who did not accept employer dismissals or refused to forfeit their right to reinstatement. According to government statistics, employers failed to comply with 79 percent of labor courts' reinstatement orders. In some cases employers did not reinstate workers to their prior positions and often failed to pay the back wages owed to them, as well as court-ordered fines. Local unions reported businesses continued to use fraudulent bankruptcies, ownership substitution, and reincorporation of companies to circumvent legal obligations to recognize newly formed or established unions, despite legal restrictions on such practices.

Although the law stipulates trade unions have an exclusive right to negotiate work conditions on behalf of workers, unions continued to assert that management promoted "solidarity associations" to discourage the formation of trade unions or to compete with existing labor unions.

b. Prohibition of Forced or Compulsory Labor

The law prohibits all forms of forced or compulsory labor. The government failed to enforce the law effectively in some cases. Reports persisted of men and women subjected to forced labor in agriculture and domestic service. Penalties ranging from two to 18 minimum monthly salaries ($665 to $6,000) were inadequate and rarely enforced. Criminal penalties for forced labor range from eight to 18 years' imprisonment. The government lacked sufficient resources (e.g., labor inspectors, vehicles, equipment) to conduct effective and regular inspection or to pursue remediation for forced labor cases. The government had specialized police and prosecutors to handle cases of human trafficking, including forced labor, although local experts reported some prosecutors lacked adequate training. In July the Public Ministry arrested two sisters who forced six children to beg in the streets for money. The case remained pending at year's end. There were also other reports of forced child labor (see section 7.c.).

Also see the Department of State's *Trafficking in Persons Report* at www.state.gov/j/tip/rls/tiprpt/.

c. Prohibition of Child Labor and Minimum Age for Employment

The law bars employment of minors below age 14, although it allows the Ministry of Labor to authorize children below age 14 to work in exceptional cases. The ministry's inspectorate reported it did not authorize any exceptions during the year.

The law prohibits persons below age 18 from working in places that serve alcoholic beverages, in unhealthy or dangerous conditions, at night, or overtime. The legal workday for persons younger than age 14 is six hours; for persons ages 14 to 17, the legal workday is seven hours.

The Ministry of Labor's Child Worker Protection Unit is responsible for enforcing restrictions on child labor and educating minors, their parents, and employers on the rights of minors. Penalties range from two to 18 minimum monthly salaries ($665 to $6,000). The government did not effectively enforce these laws, a situation exacerbated by the weakness of the labor inspection and labor court systems. The government devoted insufficient resources to prevention programs.

Child labor was a widespread problem. The NGO Conrad Project Association of the Cross estimated that the workforce included approximately one million children between ages five and 17. Most child labor occurred in rural indigenous areas of extreme poverty. The informal and agricultural sectors regularly employed children below 14, usually in small family enterprises, including in the production of broccoli, coffee, corn, fireworks, gravel, and sugar. Indigenous children also worked in street sales and as shoe shiners and bricklayer assistants.

An estimated 39,000 children, primarily indigenous girls, worked as domestic servants and were often vulnerable to physical and sexual abuse. In the Mexican border area, there were reports of forced child labor in municipal dumps and in street begging.

Also see the Department of Department of Labor's *Findings on the Worst Forms of Child Labor* at www.dol.gov/ilab/reports/child-labor/findings/.

d. Discrimination with Respect to Employment and Occupation

The law explicitly prohibits discrimination with respect to employment or occupation based on race, color, sex, religion, political opinion, national origin or citizenship, age, and disability. The government did not effectively enforce the law and related regulations.

Discrimination in employment and occupation occurred. Anecdotally, wage discrimination based on race and sex occurred often in rural areas.

e. Acceptable Conditions of Work

The law sets national minimum wages for agricultural and nonagricultural work and for work in garment factories. The minimum wage was 78.72 quetzals ($10.20) per day for agricultural and nonagricultural work and 72.36 quetzals ($9.40) per day for work in export-sector-regime factories. Minimum wage earners are due a mandatory monthly bonus of 250 quetzals ($32.50), and salaried workers receive two mandatory yearly bonuses (a Christmas bonus and a "14th month" bonus), each equivalent to one month's salary. The National Statistics Institute estimated the minimum food budget for a family of five was 3,123 quetzals ($406) per month. The basic basket for vital needs, including food and housing, was 6,242 quetzals ($810).

The legal workweek is 48 hours with at least one paid 24-hour rest period. Workers are not supposed to work more than 12 hours a day. The law provides for 12 paid annual holidays and paid vacation of 15 days after one year's work. Daily and weekly maximum hour limits do not apply to domestic workers. Workers in the formal sector receive the standard pay for a day's work for official annual holidays. Time-and-a-half pay is required for overtime work, and the law prohibits excessive compulsory overtime.

The government sets occupational health and safety standards, which were inadequate, not current for all industries, and poorly enforced. The law does not provide for the right of workers to remove themselves from situations that endangered health or safety without jeopardy to their employment.

The Ministry of Labor conducted inspections to monitor compliance with minimum wage law provisions, but resources were inadequate to enable inspectors to enforce the law, especially in the agricultural and informal sectors. The ministry employed approximately 275 labor inspectors, although many of them performed conciliation or administrative duties rather than clearly defined inspection duties.

Labor inspectors reported uncovering numerous instances of overtime abuses, but effective enforcement was undermined due to inadequate fines and labor courts' reluctance to use compulsory measures, such as increased fines and referrals to the criminal courts, to obtain compliance. Other factors contributing to the lack of effective enforcement included labor court inefficiencies, employer refusal to permit labor inspectors to enter facilities or provide access to payroll records and other documentation, and inspectors' lack of follow-up inspections in the face of such refusals. Labor inspectors were not authorized to sanction employers but had to submit alleged violations to the labor courts. Due to inefficient and lengthy court proceedings, the resolution of cases was often delayed, in many instances for years. Moreover, fines ranging from 50 to 5,000 quetzals ($6.50 to $650) were not sufficient to deter violations. Authorities often failed to investigate fully or assign responsibility for negligence. They also rarely sanctioned employers for failing to provide a safe workplace. Legislation requiring companies with more than 50 employees to provide onsite medical facilities for their workers was not enforced.

Trade union leaders and human rights groups reported that employers required workers to work overtime without legally mandated premium pay. Management often manipulated employer-provided transportation to worksites to force employees to work overtime, especially in export processing zones located in isolated areas with limited transportation alternatives. Noncompliance with minimum wage provisions in the agricultural and informal sectors was widespread. Advocacy groups estimated that the vast majority of workers in rural areas who engaged in daylong employment did not receive the wages, benefits, or social security allocations required by law. Some employers in the agricultural sector reportedly conditioned payment of minimum wage on excessive production goals that workers generally were unable to meet. According to ILO statistics, 74 percent of the workforce worked in the informal sector and outside the basic protections afforded by law.

Local unions continued to highlight and protest violations by employers who failed to pay employer and employee contributions to the national social security system despite employee contribution deductions from workers' paychecks. These violations, particularly common in export industries, resulted in limiting or denying employees' access to the public health system and reducing or underpaying workers' pension benefits during their retirement years.